AN IMMIGRANT'S ODYSSEY TO CANADA

AN IMMIGRANT'S ODYSSEY TO CANADA

STEPS AND STRATEGIES TO HELP YOU PLAN AHEAD

ERICA BURNETT

©2023 Erica Burnett

All rights reserved. No part of this publication may be reproduced, distributed, or transmitted in any form or by any means, including photocopying, recording, or other electronic or mechanical methods, without the prior written permission of the publisher, except in the case of brief quotations embodied in critical reviews and certain other noncommercial uses permitted by copyright law.

For permission requests, write to the author at ericaburnett01@yahoo.com distribution: www.odysseytocanada.com

ISBN 979-8859706471

Cover Designed: Business Startup & Marketing Solutions LLC

Printed in the United States of America and Canada

Table of Contents

ACKNOWLEDGEMENT 1
INTRODUCTION 4
Chapter 1 THE BETRAYAL 7
Chapter 2 SHATTERED DREAM 15
Chapter 3 THE RETURN HOME 19
Chapter 4 PREPARING FOR THE TRANSITION 25
Chapter 5 THE MYSTERY 29
Chapter 6 FORGIVENESS BRINGS BLESSING 35
Chapter 7 LIFE IN CANADA 39
Chapter 8 SCHOOL LIFE 45
Chapter 9 WORK OPPORTUNITIES 54
Chapter 10 THE INTERVIEWS 61
Chapter 11 DID I MAKE THE RIGHT DECISION 70
Chapter 12 DESTINY & TIME MET 77

ACKNOWLEDGEMENT

This book was written through the inspiration of the Holy Spirit, my teacher and friend—all honor and glory to you, Lord Jesus Christ.

My confidant and friend, Alecia McIntosh, was supportive when I mentioned my intention to migrate. She provided emotional and spiritual support from the inception. My mom, Nelletta McCarthy and sister, Andrea White, believed in supported and encouraged me throughout the journey. My eldest brother, Dave McCarthy, was a significant supporter and initiator of my immigration journey. His family embraced and facilitated my family throughout our transition. They cheerfully shared their space and incorporated us as an extension of their immediate family, my gorgeous sister-in-love, Donna, who beautifully decorated our homes. Donna's parents and sister also embraced us as a part of their family.

ACKNOWLEDGEMENT

My husband's family. Judy Mawoyo, the epitome of a meek and gentle spirit with wisdom and her husband, Abisha, supported us greatly. My brother-in-love, Leon Burnett, and his fantastic wife, Vennessa, were helpful and compassionate. Vennessa is one of the kindest, most considerate and sweetest people I have ever met.

I call Dominique Jordan and Shawntee Russell (Jesus' girls); they are unique, kind, loving, and helpful. These girls are Vennessa's best friends; I only got to know them when we arrived in Canada, and they became family immediately. Even when Vennessa was not around, they supported us, and our children loved them.

My friend, Sharon Nelson-Bailey, encouraged me on my first attempt to immigrate to Canada. She prayed and talked with me on those long phone calls.

Tramaine Wisdom, my dear, beloved, long-time friend and Godmother to my daughter, stood with me and my family when we needed her the most. She never ceased to put a smile on her Goddaughter's face. I love you, girl!

To my fabulous friend Trishawna Davis, it is amazing how we met while doing our Project Management Course at the University of the West Indies, Continuing Studies, Open Campus. The Lord used your voice to advise me on strategically embarking on the journey, and from this interaction, you dedicated your life to Christ Jesus. Glory to God!

ACKNOWLEDGMENT

My friends from Centennial College, with whom we interceded together for legislation to change have proven God. He changed those laws during the pandemic, and we received our Permanent Residence quickly.

I encourage those still waiting for their Permanent Residence to keep their faith. God is working. He is faithful and has not forgotten you.

Cheers to all International Students who persevered despite the challenges!

Thanks to everyone I crossed paths with on my journey to settle permanently in Canada!

Troy Burnett, my beloved husband, prayer partner and friend, has been a tower of strength. He has been my rock in everything I do and has sacrificed so much for our family. Thank you, my love.

INTRODUCTION

Take delight in the Lord and He will give you the desires of your heart. Commit everything you do to the Lord. Trust Him, and He will help you.

Psalm 37:4-5

Troy and I had birthed the desire to migrate to Canada with our children for over ten years. Time and destiny met in mid-2018 when my application to study in Canada was approved. We knew the timing was perfect as our plans quickly fell into place.

Waiting for the opportune time to do anything is never easy, especially when there is no certainty of what lies ahead.

Proceeding with God's plan for our lives, patience, prayer, preparation, perseverance, focus, and determination are vital characteristics during this season.

INTRODUCTION

I believe God orders all our steps, and if we are patient and trust Him, we will receive what He has in store for us. He cares for us so much that every detail of our lives concerns Him (Psalm 37:23-24). This includes where we should live, the people we connect with, the school we should attend, who we will marry, and the timing. He will bring all these things to pass.

Frequently, we discover or move into our purposes when faced with difficulties and are desperate for change. Discovery of gifts, interests, and talents is birthed in this season.

It is true, according to Matthew 6:33 (NLT). *Seek the Kingdom of God above all else and live righteously, and he will give you everything you need.*

God knows your desires. Be patient while He brings those desires to pass.

I got sick and tired of my routine, environment, and job. I desperately desired a change because I believed I had wings to fly but was restricted by my familiar surroundings. Most times, the best place to thrive is in unfamiliar places among unfamiliar faces.

INTRODUCTION

The desire to migrate became so strong that I began to call the things which are not as though they were (Romans 4:17).

My confidant and friend, Alecia, found it so funny that every time we were working together and as we drove past certain places, I would boldly declare that that was the last month or year that I was doing a particular thing or passing a place while living in Jamaica. I would be driving on bigger and broader roads; I would be in Canada that time next year.

We both knew the word of God and knew that there was life and death in the power of the tongue (Proverbs 18:21) and that God spoke the world into being (Psalms 33:6-9).

And it came to pass the next year! It was time for me and my family to board the plane to our new home in beautiful Canada. Hallelujah!

I would love to hear from you if you have questions or feedback. Please leave a review on Amazon or my social media pages, or at odysseytocanada@gmail.com and my website at www.odysseytocanada.com

Thank you!

CHAPTER 1
THE BETRAYAL

On July 29, 2018, when my family and I arrived at the Pearson International Airport in Canada, we were elated as a new chapter of our lives was about to begin.

My husband and I knew this was a journey of faith and trust in our Lord. We were unafraid, as we knew this was a move ordained by God.

We fell in love with Canada when we visited for the first time in fall of October 2007 for my sister-in-law Judy-Ann's wedding. We were impressed by the beauty and cleanliness of the place, and how courteous and orderly the people were.

When we returned to Jamaica, the image and fascination of Canada lingered in our minds. This was when my husband and I discussed immigration and researched the various opportunities the country offered. At that point, I signed up for a weekly newsletter from a top-rated consultant in Canada to learn more about migration. We received tips and kept abreast of the immigration process. An assessment was done with the company, but to our disappointment, we needed to be qualified to sponsor ourselves. A well-known consultant was hired on the way forward, and we inquired of the school route venture. Advise was given that other countries could go with their families, except for Jamaicans. Separating our family was not an option; the news was disheartening, so Canada remained an unfulfilled desire for a while. As life continued, we waited for the dream to become reality. In 2014, migration grew even more robust, and a new level of research was pursued for the journey.

During that period, only a few places in Jamaica were authorized to advise on Canadian immigration. At first, no progress was made but it was a Television advertisement. Troy saw the information regarding Jamaicans migrating to Canada. I happily registered for the program and began the process, which involved doing a Customer Service course at the City and Guild level (This is a British Examination). The school that offered the opportunity did not take into consideration if the participants had tertiary education, everyone were required to do this course. After completing the course, there was a big graduation ceremony. The next process involved being assigned to a so-called immigration company that was legitimately registered locally. The success story of a few tradesmen, which the local organization processed, gave the program creditability. It was later discovered that they didn't have a connection with different categories of Canadian employers, such as in the business studies field, which most of the participants were qualified for.

It was hard to think this program would not work because their partners from Canada came to Jamaica to do job fairs and training, even offered CPR certifications. At one of their information sessions, an immigration lawyer was in attendance for question and answer session and to provide information on the immigration pathway. These sessions were held at hotels, and everything seemed organized and was done professionally.

The participants of the program outnumbered by far the Canadian employers. The demand was so great that the Canadian organizers inquired why so many persons wanted to leave Jamaica. Of course, people expressed different reasons, including crime, corruption, and economic climate.

Being an assertive person who had already obtained a Canadian visa, I suggested that I visit Canada to have direct contact with the companies offering employment and I could finish the immigration process in Canada. To my surprise, local and Canadian authorities agreed and I went to Alberta, Canada. Before I went, I sought the Lord, and He spoke to me through Psalm 16:5 - 6. It resonated with me.

The land you have given me is a pleasant land. What a wonderful inheritance. I was confident that I was meant to go! The local immigration recruiter requested a specific amount of money. I negotiated, and he would receive the funds upon completing the process.

I travelled on my visitor's visa in October 2014 with a fully paid trip, flight and hotel accommodations included. Two Jamaican men from the skilled workers program were on the same flight but we never met them until the recruiter picked us up at the airport.

Our hosts were friendly; we were fed and transported to the hotel. The next day, I went to the recruiter's office and began job hunting. The men already knew their employers; the recruiter took them shopping to get their work gears.

The next day, I was pleasantly surprised by the new and beautiful scenery. The air was fresh; greenery was all around. It was pleasant to look at. I immediately fell in love with my new environment. There were massive stretches of land; the place was big and beautiful! I recognized that the Fall in Alberta looked different from Ontario, at least in the city of Red Deer where I stayed. Many trees did not change colors but maintained their lush greenery.

The recruiter's office was spacious and modern. Upon entering, I was welcomed and introduced to everyone. I was given a computer to review data with hundreds of employers to apply for jobs, but I realized that the data needed to be updated.

By this time, I recognized that the recruiter was not partnering with employers they knew to fill job vacancies but was merely using some leads from a general job database to fill positions.

While going through the data the recruiter provided, I did no interviews. The recruiter invited me to a lunch interview with one of their friends, who wanted an Administrative Assistant. That was my first time doing a lunch interview, not that it was different from any other office interview, but I found it distracting to be questioned while eating. I did my best anyway because I was anxious to secure a job so my family could join me.

Ultimately, my interview was unsuccessful because the employer said I did not seem interested in the job. I was surprised to hear that remark. I laughed because I needed a job; why wouldn't I be interested?

After that, I continued visiting the recruiter's office to do my job search while my hotel accommodation was being paid for.. I didn't have sufficient money for daily expenses; therefore, I would reserve food for dinner after the hotel's complimentary breakfast. I wouldn't have to worry about lunch because they usually provided lunch.

Job fairs are popular in Canada, this is usually where numerous employers gather in a location to recruit workers. I was invited to attend two of them in nearby cities. The drive to these fairs was at least two hours from the recruiter's office. In all fairness, they tried tirelessly to help me find jobs, but it was impossible because the law for hiring non-skilled temporary workers had changed three months before I had arrived in Canada.

I became disappointed and hopeless as I pursued the job search because I needed a Labour Market Impact Assessment (LMIA) a document employers in Canada need before hiring a foreign worker. This document shows that there is a need for foreign worker to fill the job, it also shows there is no Canadian worker or Permanent Resident available to do the job.. The only way I could be hired was if I got a (LMIA). Unfortunately, I could not get a LMIA.

The Jamaican recruiting company that sent me to Canada was contacted to inform that the Canadian recruiter were not partnering directly with employers to fill vacancies. They used a general database to locate jobs. He was in denial and shocked but did nothing about it but my relationship with the Canadian recruiter to find work continued.. While I was in Canada, the overseas company were still visiting

Jamaica to host job fairs; the Immigration Lawyer was also present on these trips. I called the participants of the program to share with them that they should take back their money because things were not how they made it seem. The Canadian recruiter did not have jobs for them. A few went back to get a refund; some did not.

The Canadian recruiters were a relatively new company. I sincerely believed that they had good intentions at the inception of the process, but changing immigration law to bring in non skilled foreign workers impacted their business.

They needed to be more transparent and communicate what they were doing to the Jamaican company instead of continuing to take their money and enjoying free vacations in Jamaica. They were disingenuous and gave false hope to the Jamaican company and the program participants.

I was blessed to have my sister-in-law Judy and her husband living in another city around an hour away; sometimes they visited, or I would go to them on the weekends.

I remember one weekend, when I went by my in-laws', it snowed. I was very excited because it was my first time experiencing snow. It was a fantastic experience, playing, touching and tasting the snow. It felt so peaceful and therapeutic, watching it fall from the sky. To see all of this ice accumulated was thrilling and I enjoyed every moment of it. That weekend the recruiters dropped me off at my in-laws' to spend the weekend. They were to pick me back up on the following Monday when they returned to that city, but I had yet to hear back from them after a week. I was in shock and embarrassed at the same time. This wasn't the plan. How could they have been so evil? I felt betrayed.

I remained with Judy and extended my vacation at work in Jamaica while I pursued my job search for another two months in Canada, hoping that I might get an employer to sponsor me with a LMIA. I went on interviews to work as a Front Desk Clerk, and Customer Service Representative but those were not LMIA jobs. The employers were interested in hiring me, but due to the fact that the positions were not for skillled workers.

CHAPTER 2
SHATTERED DREAM

Life is never perfect. Sometimes we have to make temporary decisions that affect the normalcy of our lives. I have never taken a long trip without my children and husband but in this case, I had temporarily left my son Nathan at seventeen month-old and daughter Gihannah-Kay at seven-year-old. The thought devastated me, however, I knew they would be well taken care of by Troy, my sister, their paternal grandfather, and my mom.

I had to find a way to feel close to my children while I was away, so I took a piece of their clothing with me to have their scent so I slept with their clothes every night just to have that feeling of closeness to them.

Gihannah-Kay's birthday came while I was in Canada, that morning I woke up overwhelmed with tears and cried like there was no tomorrow. At that point, I understood what it meant for someone's heart to hurt because I felt that heartache with only the thought of my princess celebrating her birthday without me. I was emotionally wrecked that day and was comforted by Judy who encouraged me that we would be together soon.

One Thursday morning while at my in-laws' home, each time I visited the kitchen, I heard a voice saying, "There goes Gihannah-Kay's school." It was an elementary school facing their home. I asked," Lord, if this is you speaking to me, please confirm that it is you." I forgot about that experience until the Saturday when we returned from shopping. I remember Judy-Ann's husband mentioned, "They are having a fair at Gihannah-Kay's School." (by him saying this, I believed that was the confirmation from the Lord because he did not know of my experience a couple of days prior when I heard the voice of the Lord. This encounter motivated me to continue my job search positively. My brother Dave, who lives in another Province, connected me with people he knew who could assist with my job search, but to no avail. It was four days before Christmas; most businesses were closed for the holidays, still, I had not found a job. Time was quickly running out on me as my vacation would soon expire. I was devastated that I had not found work! How could this be?

God said He had given me the land! (Canada) He told me Gihannah-Kay's school was here in Alberta!

One morning in mid-December, I woke up crying inconsolably. I felt neglected by God! I felt like he had failed me! How could I receive so many confirmations to come to Alberta, receive more confirmations while here, and then the opportunity to stay was not materializing? I felt so disappointed. Judy was home from work that day and offered great support. She prayed with me, took me to the mall, and later watched a movie. That took my mind off my sorrows and brought comfort.

Then came Christmas! When we went to church, my heart was ripped apart again when I saw other children beautifully dressed and participating in the service. All I could envision at that moment were my children on the stage. I tried to hold back my tears, but they kept flowing down my face. I was successful in not sobbing loudly because I didn't want to draw attention to myself. This was my first Christmas without my family, and I vowed that would never happen again. The pain was too much to bear.

I communicated with my family, which made me smile because they enjoyed their Christmas, which they spent with their father's family. It was exciting for them to see many of their cousins who they got to play with.

I told Troy that at the beginning of the new year, I would visit one more company to check if they would hire me located around ten minutes from my in-law's home. I took the bus and walked in the high snow and cold for around twenty minutes because the bus did not go to that location. I spoke with the employer looking to hire a Printer, who told me the hard truth. "Ma'am, unless we cannot find a Printer in Canada and prove that to the government, we cannot hire you. (What he meant was that I needed a LMIA, the special work permit). I already knew this, but it hit home strongly because I knew I had to return to Jamaica without my mission's success. I felt at that time that my dream to emigrate to Canada was shattered.

On my way home from the company, I called Troy and told him it would not work out for me to get a job. I had to come home. He said it was okay. He told me that the entire day before, a song by a famous gospel singer kept playing in his head and said, " What if it does not work the first time? Will you still trust me?"

I called the Immigration Lawyer who worked with the Canadian recruiter and told her all that had happened to me, how the recruiters abandoned me at my in-laws. She was livid and vowed to cut all ties with them; she paid my airfare to return to Jamaica.

CHAPTER 3
THE RETURN HOME

I was a month into my stay with Judy, who kept reminding me that "God sent me to spy out the land." (Canada) I did not want to hear that. I could not understand why obtaining a job in Canada was not working because I had asked the Lord if I should go, and he had said yes; therefore, I was expecting things to work out now!

On different occasions, while in Canada, at the bus stop or library or walking along the road, I would decree and declare in the atmosphere that

God had given me this land; it was pleasant. My husband, me and my children, and their children would inherit the land. My generation would be blessed in the land of Canada.

A new excitement arose when my flight was booked to return to Jamaica! I was going to see my babies; I was going home! The sadness left me. No one knew I was returning to Jamaica except my husband, mom, and sister. I will never forget the joy on my children's faces when I "bussed in the yard." (meaning entered the home) Troy's parents and brother were there. Everyone was surprised. The children ran to me, hugged me, and shouted, "Mommy!" Oh, what joy filled my heart! I was reunited with my family! They laughed; we kissed and held each other tightly for a long while. Nothing was better than that feeling for me and my family. We were happy!

I brushed off all disappointments and returned to my job. Sadly, it was time to return to the same old routine I hated. I was happy to see my friends and some of my coworkers.

I went back like Mrs. Santa Clause, bearing small gifts; after all, I came back from a "foreign" country! I parcelled gifts, such as pens and sweets from the many hotels I stayed at. My friends and co-workers were so grateful and excited to see me return from "vacation."

I appreciated my job and was thankful for it after I went to a foreign country and could not secure one, and I could have returned to work two and a half months later. The days seemed so long and did not go by quickly enough. There were several adjustments at work as the company was restructuring, bringing about a lot of tension and uncertainty. I needed something to distract me from all that was happening around me.

In previous years, my "side hustle" was visiting the United States to purchase clothing, shoes, and accessories for retail. I later returned to my "retail hustle" (my backup informal business), only sourcing my products locally this time. (My previous place of employment was huge and had several branches). This was easy because I was serving people that I was in contact with daily. My mom and sister Andrea were loyal customers; anyone that I came into contact with became my customer.

Things were going well until the morning of May 9, 2014. The Lord prompted me to read Mark 6:30-44 (NLT). I remember the date because I marked it in my Bible.

It was the story of Jesus feeding five thousand. Verses 41-44 resonated with me. Jesus took the five loaves and two fish, looked up toward heaven, and blessed them. Then, breaking the loaves into pieces, he kept giving the bread to the disciples so they could distribute it to the people. He also divided the fish for everyone to share. They all ate as much as they wanted, and afterward, the disciples picked up twelve baskets of leftover bread and fish. A total of 5,000 men and their families.

I did not understand why I was led to read that passage, but I did it! As soon as I arrived in the parking lot at work, I was prompted to read another scripture. 2 Kings 4. Elisha helps a poor widow. Verses 1-7 stood out to me.

I reflected on the scriptures, trying to contextualize what the Lord was saying..

As if those scriptures were not enough, at lunchtime, I was prompted to read John 6: 1- 13.. Jesus feeds five thousand. I was convinced by now that the Lord was talking to me about multiplication and telling me to use whatever I had in my hand. (Meaning talents and available resources). I was elated and expectant of the doors and opportunities that the Lord would open in my life.

The next time I went shopping, I found a location I had never visited and was pleasantly surprised! Various cardigans of different colours, sizes, and styles attracted me. I was pleased to see how they were reasonably priced and purchased a few of each to test how well they would do on the market. They sold so quickly that I had to go back to get more. These were easy sales because of the quality, trend, and reasonable prices.

Clients purchased one of each color and sometimes ordered other colors for my next sale. The market expanded tremendously! I was now going to several locations, including offices outside my usual spots. I remember placing an advertisement on Facebook about the cardigans I had for sale.

Someone I hardly knew contacted me and inquired if I could come to her location to sell the staff there. She worked at a University and arranged for me to visit her office. I went with a suitcase full of cardigans, and only left with two! I was in awe!

I thought there were still kind-hearted people in this world. She became a Sales Agent for me. I would deliver the cardigans to her according to the demand. She continued to help me for a long time. The cardigan market never dried up. I became known as the "Cardigan Girl" or "Cardigan Lady." I continued selling other apparel, but this became my niche.

I was living in the manifestation of the scriptures the Lord had me read on May 9, 2014. All honor and glory to Lord Jesus.

Being productive and personal development is essential. I have an insatiable appetite for growth! Whatever growth looks like, I embrace it because I despise stagnancy.

I decided to return to school after doing a S.W.O.T. analysis on myself. I learnt of this assessment in previous Marketing courses taken. It means assessing strengths, weaknesses, opportunities and threats (external factors) a business faces. Preparation for any opportunity within my company or anywhere it produced itself was essential since my dream of going to Canada appeared behind me.

Although I enjoyed learning, I was not excited to return to school because this meant less time with my family, additional expenses, several years of commitment, and less downtime. I discussed my desire with Troy, who supported my return to school.

Even with his support, I was still determining how to handle a full-time job or part-time business—even though my clients were easy to find. Shopping for my products was time-consuming, sometimes including several weekly trips to the locations because of how quickly the sales went.

I decided I would succeed with discipline, commitment, determination, support from my family and God's help.

CHAPTER 4
PREPARING FOR THE TRANSITION

Summer of 2017, we decided to go to Canada for a vacation. The love for that beautiful, clean country lingered when we arrived, but I was in vacation mode. My mindset was just to visit family, shop, and have fun. While staying with my brother Dave, one day, he said, "Sis, I took the liberty of booking an appointment with the major's office to see how they could help you to immigrate here." I said, "Okay, no problem. I will go, but I have researched all the possible ways, and the only other way we could use is the school route, which is not an option because it is costly, and I am already in school in Jamaica."

When we went to the major's office, we received the same information as I told Dave. I was not disappointed because I already knew the answer. I was on two weeks of vacation leave, so I returned to work and left my family in Canada to enjoy the rest of their trip. After I returned home, unbeknownst to me, Troy and Dave went to a College half an hour from Dave's home to make inquiries about attending College. When Troy telephoned and informed me of the school's requirements, I told him, "Good for you and Dave! You can do the studies."

On the return of my family from vacation, Troy brought catalogues and reading materials from the school. We discussed ways we could make the transition. Our conversation amazed me, and the research recommenced on how we could fund this costly venture.

I communicated with the University I attended and queried how to complete my studies in Canada since Troy was not interested in studying there. I continued with other research for the journey to be successful and received advice from a few people, including two participants from the program I was a part of. They were studying in Canada, and another friend in Jamaica, who was familiar with the process, told me of the mistakes other applicants made that caused them not to be successful. My friend Trishawna showed me how to save the proof of funds Immigration required strategically.

Troy and I met with the Immigration Consultant to discuss the school route and how to relocate together as a family. We received a favourable response.

PREPARING FOR THE TRANSITION

My college application was submitted by the end of 2017, and I awaited a reply from the college by the end of January to early February of the following year. While waiting for my application's approval, we continued our groundwork. Our analysis included the average cost of rent in my brother's neighbourhood, transportation costs to get to school, and the time it would take to travel to school on public transportation. I kept abreast of the immigration policy laws, as those laws in Canada change frequently, the type of records our children would need to maintain their status there if their schools required immigration records for their admittance and all the necessary things we could think of to ensure our venture would be without eventualities. I maintained close communication with Dave and updated him on our progress. We secured advice from anyone who could assist in preparing for the transition.

Financial planning was a huge part of our preparation as we had obligations to fulfil in Jamaica and the expenses we anticipated in pursuing our dream in Canada.

We monitored the exchange rate and purchased the Canadian Dollar at the cheapest rates.

Eventually we were able to purchase the amount we needed to take with us. The maximum cash allowed for each family was $10,000 CDN or its equivalent as an international traveller.

If more than is taken then you have to declare it when you arrived in Canada.

We were prayerful about our intended plans which we kept close to our hearts, involving only our support system and parents who would be impacted by our move, simply because it was wise to announce plans only when they came into being.

Proverbs 16:9 (NLT) states we can make our plans, but the LORD determines our steps. So, why not wait and see how the Lord would determine our steps before making an announcement.

Adjusting to new environments maybe difficult for some children. Therefore having conversations of what to expect during the change is vital for their sanity and well being.

Troy and I discussed how we would prepare our children mentally and emotionally for our expected journey. We decided to tell them about the different weather conditions they would experience, different cultures they will interact with in school they should never feel pressured to adapt other cultures but be respectful to them, embrace and be proud of their own culture, be confident, uphold their morals, remember the values taught to them and aspire to do their best at all times.

CHAPTER 5
THE MYSTERY

It was mid-February 2018, and we had not heard from Centennial College. I contacted the Immigration Consultant to enquire why there was a delay in hearing from the school regarding my application for my Graduate Diploma? He did not provide a valid reason, so I called the College to investigate why I had not yet received an acceptance letter for the course. When I called the Administrator for International Studies she was often out of the office or unavailable for a call. I persisted in calling until I spoke with her. When I inquired about my application for the Post Graduate Corporate Sales and Account Management course, she informed me that she could not find my application and that the program I applied for was full. When I asked her the program's name, she told me a different name from the one I applied for. I could not believe what I was hearing! She was looking for the incorrect information! How could this be?

How could they err! The program I had applied for was a Postgraduate Diploma, and she was giving me information for a certificate program! She eventually found the correct application, apologized and told me she would email me my acceptance letter to study at the College. A couple of days later, she followed through with her commitment.

After misplacing my application to study at the College, I considered what if I had not called. Would I be waiting indefinitely? What did I pay the Consultant for?

I was happy I received the acceptance letter. I could now apply for my study permit. I now had all the required documents:

- Proof of acceptance letter
- Proof of identity
- Proof of financial funds

The Immigration Consultant submitted my application, and Troy and I patiently awaited the approval.

While the Canadian Embassy processed my study permit, we strategized when we would end the tenure at our jobs. We decided to take our vacation time then resign from our positions. Since my company was restructuring, I had the option to retire. I learned about this through a union delegate whom I casually spoke with. I was glad to hear this news because I could take advantage of retaining my salary until I chose to retire at the end of my vacation.

Suddenly, before my permit was approved the Organization that I worked with informed the staff members that anyone considering applying for early retirement had to do so by a specific date. I was shocked when I read the memo because the date the Organization was suggesting to submit the application for retirement was four months before the time I had planned to retire. Anxiety stepped in and I wondered how we would finance our bills during that time? Troy and I needed that money from my job to purchase more Canadian dollars! The visa was not yet processed, but I could not allow this opportunity for early retirement to pass by! I spoke with our support system, who advised me to accept the opportunity. When I told my husband, he disagreed, as he was concerned about how we would survive financially until the time we planned to leave. Time was not on our hand to discuss the matter fully because I had to submit this application in four days.

I told him God did not work in confusion, so we needed to seek the Lord independently for direction then come back together to share what the Lord revealed to us. He agreed.

The following morning, I sought the Lord regarding his direction. He answered me immediately! through Mark 11: 23-25 (NLT).

"I tell you the truth, you can say to this mountain, may you be lifted up and thrown into the sea," and it will happen. But you must really believe it will happen and have no doubt in your heart. I tell you, you can pray for anything, and if you believe that you've received it, it will be yours. But when you are praying, first forgive anyone you are holding a grudge against, so that your Father in heaven will forgive your sins, too."

I was confident the answer was yes! I was at peace and joyful. My husband waited until after the weekend to give me his answer; he said I could do it. He got the peace. We agreed we could move forward to submit my application for retirement, which I completed immediately after the memo was published.

My managers, friends at work, and co-workers were shocked, except for my confidant Alecia, who had been walking the journey with me from my first attempt to migrate to Canada. After returning from my vacation in 2017, she heard me making declarations about doing things for the last time while residing in Jamaica and was aware of the entire process.

My application for my retirement required the approval of a manager's signature before submission to the Human Resources Department but all the managers were on a training course and I was acting in the position of manager so when they saw me arrive at the training center, they were astonished. So I had to explain the reason for my presence. I spoke with them simultaneously, and they began asking, "why was I leaving?"They did not expect this? What was I going to do? "The general answer I gave them was that my season at the Organization had ended, and I was exploring new opportunities.

This answer came across, to many, as a puzzle. My co-workers wanted more answers, and the questions continued, but the answer remained the same. Many thought I would do my "side hustle" full-time and looked at me with disdain because I was leaving my executive job to turn "higgler." One person said, "So, you are really leaving your work to sell clothes?" She said it in Patois, so it sounded more intense. I listened and entertained them, asking what was wrong with that. I would have my own business.

Some thought I was lying and were presumptuous enough to ask if I had plans I should tell them what they were. In your dreams, I thought.

I left the Organization I worked for sixteen years in March 2018. Many conveyed best wishes, but my department leaders did not even buy a "bulla cake with some water," nor did the staff come together to say thanks for the service I rendered or best wishes. I was not surprised or angry. I thought about how unvalued I was to them.

When I visited my ex-organization to conduct sales with staff members, some ridiculed me and said, "Why did you leave the job? What are you doing with yourself?" Another said, "Do you want the work back, don't you?" and continued to say I could ask for my job back.

I laughed in my mind at these pathetic people. It is good to hear what is in people's hearts when they don't know your next move because man speaks out of the abundance of the heart.

I like the way Luke 6:45 (NLT) puts it:

A good person produces good things from the treasury of a good heart, and an evil person produces evil things from the treasury of an evil heart. What you say flows from what is in your heart.

The same week I was migrating to Canada, I went to my old office to do business and told my ex-coworkers I was relocating. The news brought further shock to a lot of them. My mockers were more respectful of me.

CHAPTER 6
FORGIVENESS BRINGS BLESSING

One of the first thoughts I faced before retiring was finding a job for the remaining months in Jamaica. I was presumptuous enough to give the Lord a deadline to help me find that job the first Monday after I left my previous job. I contacted people I knew that could help me find a job however, that did not materialize.

A few weeks after I retired, one morning, I had a strong urge to kneel before the Lord. After I knelt, I was quiet for some time, and then I was prompted to open my bible; it opened on John 11:40 (NLT). Jesus responded, "Didn't I tell you that you would see God's glory if you believe?"

I was in awe when I read this scripture verse and felt like the Lord reprimanded me. All I could say was, "Wow, I am sorry; yes, Lord!" At that moment, I knew I should be still and trust the process. The Lord would provide; I didn't need to search for a job.

At the end of my first month off work, I made my exact paycheck as I would if I was still employed to my Organization. It was unbelievable!

I was motivated by the support and the money I made in the first month. and enthusiastically continued with my sales. I was given help from staff members from my previous Organization, friends and families. The support was astonishing. I was grateful that the Lord provided all of these people I refer to as my destiny helpers for that period.

I looked forward to the semester at school ending and spent time visiting extended family members while waiting for my study permit approval. I felt so good to be free from a nine-to-five job.

One morning, Troy and I were praying together; a part of the prayer was, Lord if anyone has ought against us unknowingly, please show it to us. Within minutes, the Lord showed me someone who thought I was responsible for an unfavourable outcome that happened to her. I called the person immediately, but the phone went unanswered several times. I persisted in calling until I reached her. When the person came on the phone, I told her not to be alarmed I was calling.

I wanted to apologize for any hurt I might have caused her and for us to let go of the past and move forward. Before I could finish speaking to her, she was receptive and agreed.

The following Sunday, (I was visiting a Church because my friend Trishawna decided to become a Christian and wanted a smaller church to attend rather than my home Church. She accepted the Lord as her Saviour, got baptized and is still serving as a Sunday school teacher at the same Church). In the middle of the service, the prophet said, "The lady in the black and white dress" (I was that lady), "because you have released someone, the Lord is giving you your breakthrough." I was shocked! I then remembered the call I had made during the week to ask for forgiveness. I was amazed at how God was working in my life.

Mark 11:25 But when you are praying, first forgive anyone you are holding a grudge against, so that your Father in heaven will forgive your sins, too.

The following Monday morning, I received an email from the Immigration Consultant that my study permit was approved! This news called for jubilation!

The reason I had to return to Jamaica now made sense. The Lord had brought me back so I could retire from my job. My faith in Him increased significantly because God never does anything to harm us. He proved that when He speaks, it will come to pass, not necessarily in my timing but in his time. He always has a plan for those who call upon him for help.

We began sharing the exciting news with our extended family members, neighbours, friends, and children. Our daughter Gihannah began to cry when we told her we were moving to Canada. In tears, she asked, "What about Grandma?" and ran to call her on the phone.

She was very close to my mom; after she spoke with her, she stopped crying and was receptive to the news. I was happy that she did. On the other hand, Nathan, only five years old, clung to me for the rest of our time in Jamaica.

The memory of leaving him for a few months when he was younger was still fresh in his mind.

We arranged for both children to spend quality time with their friends before they left. The closure was necessary for them.

CHAPTER 7
LIFE IN CANADA

The journey of migrating temporarily or permanently can come with stress, anxiety, and uncertainties. Therefore, careful planning, wisdom, and due diligence are essential for the seamless journey.

I arranged for my family to stay temporarily with Dave. Our accommodation would be for a reasonable time. He offered to care for us financially until we found our home. We were grateful for the offer.

Clear communication and boundaries are essential to avoid unrealistic expectations and conflicts with host families or friends. It should never be assumed that we can inconvenience them by staying with them for an extended period. It does not matter how close the relations are. We should respect their personal space.

We started house hunting from the minute we arrived, not only because of the time we agreed to stay with my brother and his family but because our address would determine where our children would attend school. Property owners usually require a credit report, so we sought to rent from informal property owners. We knew this would limit our search, especially since we were a family of four. However, as the word of God declares, we should "come boldly before the throne room," and that's what we did before we left Jamaica. One such prayer included, "Lord, we know there must be someone in Canada with an unoccupied house who can help make our stay comfortable. We were happy that our search for a place was short, and we stayed with my brother and his family for one month less than the time agreed. Judy, as we affectionately call her, was visiting from Alberta and was staying with one of her cousins.

One morning, we were having breakfast at Dave's house when Judy joined us and casually mentioned that she asked a family member if Troy and his family could stay in an unoccupied house they had. Judy said they had offered us to stay for free, but she had asked them to make it official and charge us a small rental fee. Judy mentioned the amount charged, and we could easily pay up to six months' rent.

I exclaimed, "What did you say? That is fantastic news!" Donna, Dave's wife, was grateful and cried tears of joy. Troy and I looked at each other in amazement. It was unknown to us that his family had this place.

We were excited to see the house! It was a beautiful and fully furnished townhouse. We accepted and moved into the house at the beginning of the school year. Our children's school was within walking distance, ten minutes from home. I was thirty minutes from my College on the GO bus, which took me to the school premises in front of the main building. Although travelling on this bus was a costly mode of transportation, it was more efficient than taking two buses at a cheaper cost to the College. I was anxious to travel on the GO bus because it looked exciting and had an upstairs and downstairs. Passengers only embarked and disembarked on this bus at designated stops. I was once more in awe of God's goodness towards my family.

I looked forward to Orientation Day; it was exciting to see many Jamaicans. I noticed that some were volunteers while others were new students. We exchanged phone numbers and formed a WhatsApp group to support each other. We understood that any information shared would be helpful as we had different situations and were open to gathering information. I am still friends with some girls, including Donna, Nekeisha and Nastacia.

I was impressed by how huge the college was and equipped with remarkable modern amenities.

Toronto is known as the melting pot due to the diversification of nationalities. The campus was predominantly Indian; there was only one Jamaican in my class, Shara, and I took her under my wing as a little sister.

Our class consisted of a small mixture of nationalities, including Mexicans, Brazilians, Africans, Columbians, and Chinese. There were no domestic students in my class for the first semester.

As a full-time student, I expected my classes to be consecutive; instead the classes were scheduled for various times during the day. A class might be scheduled in the morning and another at 8 PM. It was difficult for some students who wanted to utilize the twenty hours given by Immigration to work and so those students were only seen in class at test time because they had to work to pay their bills. It is vital to have the required funds that immigration suggests for living expenses to avoid financial stress. Most students worked for minimum wage; it was only sufficient for pocket money. The students who did not prepare financially struggled the most.

The classes were three hours long. The lectures were manageable, but the assignments were burdensome. There was always an assignment, group work, or a test—school was extremely hectic. Managing a family and completing online school at the University in Jamaica was exhausting. I had to practice excellent time-management skills. There was no time for a social life; I had to prioritize communicating with my parents, siblings and close friends in Jamaica since I was always working on assignments.

Adjusting to school and my new environment took time, as it demanded keen attention. I had to learn to follow instructions and directions to get to my classes, navigate the campus, and communicate with my classmates, as English was not their first language.

In Jamaica, we referred to the teachers as lecturers, but in Canada, as professors. The library became my second home as I used it frequently to complete assignments and avoid distractions at home.

One evening, on my way home from school, I took the wrong bus because it had the same number as my regular bus; the distinguishing factor was a letter I had missed. When I realized I was on the wrong bus, I went to the driver and asked how I could get home from that direction. He advised me to wait until he got to the terminus, which was around forty-five minutes from the college. When we got to the terminus, I didn't feel that stupid because two other people had done the same thing. He directed us to a bus that would take us to our destination. I got home exceptionally late that evening.

In Canada, depending on an older sibling's age, they can stay up to a particular time with their younger sibling. Gihannah could watch Nathan without adult supervision for up to two hours. This alleviated our having to pay for child care.

CHAPTER 8
SCHOOL LIFE

Gihannah and Nathan were accepted in the same school Gihannah went into Grade Six while Nathan went into Senior Kindergarten. They missed the first week of school because the school district needed more immigration documents, even though the website stated that my study permit was sufficient to admit them. Dave had to take us to one of the borders to the U.S., which was a three hour drive away, to get a study permit for them. The other option was applying online, which would take a long time. The immigration officer was very cooperative . He explained to us that they offered that service only on specific days, but he would oblige since he was a dad, and he wouldn't want his children to be out of school.

Once this was sorted out the children settled comfortably into school a week later. Gihannah was apprehensive; she felt it would be awkward to join late because the students would have already started building friendships. We encouraged her not to worry she would okay. On the other hand, Nathan had no problems with the delayed start. It was more time at home for him to be entertained on his electronic device.

At the first parent night, a month after school started, we were elated by their teachers' reactions. The teachers reported that they were well-mannered, helpful, responsible, and intelligent. Nathan's teachers said he had assisted them with some of the children during reading time. Gihannah had helped in every area of her class. They were both given awards the first month of school; Nathan came home with a certificate for respect, while Gihannah received one for kindness. Almost every month, they came home with a certificate for good characteristic skills.

Our children made us proud! They excelled in school.

At the beginning of the next school year, we decided to have Nathan attend French Immersion school because he needed more challenging work as he had mastered most of what was taught before leaving school in Jamaica. During the first years of French Immersion, bilingualism is achieved by providing basic curriculum entirely in French up to grade two to give the opportunity for non-franophone students to become bilingual.

Before making the change Troy and I consulted with Nathanès principal, and she agreed that attending French Immersion school would be best for him. We were not bothered that we only spoke English and did not know French because the school provided adequate resources to support parents and children.

I found that many Caribbean parents thought the Canadian school system was not as rigorous as their home countries and became agitated because they perceived it not to be as challenging. I observed that the Canadian school system was mainly focused on improving their motor and conflict resolution skills through play and communication, while the Jamaican school system focused primarily on academics with little play.

I embraced the Canadian school system, except for yoga and sexual education classes and provided additional study material outside of school hours. They would advance to high school in the community they reside in and upon completion of high school progress to university or college.

Gihannah-Kay shares her experience below:

When I was younger, I always wanted to explore and travel the world. God gave me the opportunity to do so. One of the places I travelled became my home. Visiting Canada was an exciting venture. I remember asking my parents to take me back since I was only two years old when I first went, so it was a trip I always wanted to take. In 2017, I vacationed there and got the full experience of the country. I met my cousins and some of my aunts and uncles' friends. When I had to leave, I was sad, but I knew I would return because my uncle Leon was engaged to be married the following year and Dad and Nathan were a part of the wedding party.

A few months before we arrived in Canada for the wedding, my parents told Nathan and I were migrating to Canada; my first thought was my Grandma I cried because I did not want to leave her behind. Before we left Jamaica, we spent much time together with Grandma. When I migrated to Canada, I was excited because I would experience the different weather, and be in a new environment. Living with my cousin, aunt, and uncle was a fun time because I had never done it before.

The school culture in Jamaica was different from what I had to embrace in Canada. I could walk to school because it was much closer to home. I got opportunities such as representing my school at leadership conferences and working with special needs kids (which was one my favorite experiences) and especially being their reading buddy gave me a connection with them.

The COVID 19 pandemic surfaced in 2020 and changed the remaining years of my middle school experience, but it was still great. I was selected valedictorian, which I never thought I would receive because I only joined the school in 2018, just three years before I graduated. I am very thankful for my teachers in Jamaica and Canada. My Jamaican school years were fundamental, and my Canadian teachers embraced me and expressed confidence in my abilities. They did not give up on me.

Troy and I were delighted when we learned Gihannah was selected as valedictorian in the year 2020. She was awarded the Ontario Principal's Council Award for Student Leadership. Due to COVID-19, the school did not host an in-person graduation ceremony but opted to do an online ceremony.

Gihannah was supported by her immediate family, extended family and friends who joined the on-line ceremony. Immediately after graduation, she was surprised with a motorcade parade through the community, honking horns with congratulatory posters.

Despite the Covid 19 restrictions, she and her friends were treated to dinner and photo shoots.

The Weather

****The children adjusted to the cold weather phenomenally. We often had to insist they dress in warm clothes; it seemed they were never cold! I dreaded the cold and was overdressed sometimes, but I preferred being warm. I learned the hard way to adequately cover my throat and head after I contracted a bad cold the first fall. Being an island girl, it was difficult sometimes to dress in layers, a scarf, mittens, a winter jacket, thick socks, and boots. Dressing like this took some time to adapt to.

The weather changes so quickly from one extreme to another in the twinkle of an eye. It varies from hot to cold, bright sunshine to a thunderstorm, sun to freezing rain, and not snowing to snow. I adjusted well to the weather as I was mentally prepared, but I missed the warmth of Jamaica's sunshine. I became so appreciative of the sun and welcomed the sunlight each day. Many people fall into depression due to lack of sunshine it is vital to get sufficient sunshine and consume Vitamin D to reduce depression.

During the winter, the days are short, and the nights are long and start getting dark as early as 4 p.m.. and 6 p.m., it is like midnight. Winter officially begins in mid-December and ends in mid-March. I have experienced seeing flurries—that is very light snow—even up to late April. During the winter, animals hibernate and reappear in spring. The birds leave to go south to warmer climates, and so do some retirees called snowbirds. Deciduous trees do not have any leaves. Unfortunately, this season is the longest.

Heavy, warm jackets are worn during this time. It is essencial to be active and interact with people to maintain good mental health. Many international students without families suffered from depression and loneliness during winter; they gravely missed their families—for some, the season represented darkness. Imagine always being with your family in warm weather and adjusting to being alone and cold. Therefore, becoming a part of a community, whether it is a church, social club, or recreational center, is recommended because it is easier with support to cope in this season.

I love and appreciate each seasons. Winter represented a time of rest and solitude, bonding time with my family. We had a fair balance of visiting with Dave and his family, having Shawntee and Dominque, Leon and Vennessa over braving, at times we braved the cold and went to movies, restaurants and other events. Canada has many recreational centers in neighbourhoods where children and adults utilize these facilities for entertainment and sporting activities.

The winter is exciting for Canadians who love to ski and ice skate. Children, as well as adults, love to go tobogganing. My family and I enjoyed this activity. (Tobogganing uses a sled to go down a hill or slope for recreation).

The children were very excited about the first snowfall and played a lot in it, we walked to the park in the snow. It was a great bonding time for the family. I am sure it was evident to anyone who saw us that it was our first snowfall; we didn't care what anyone thought. We were living in the moment.

Like myself, many people love spring. It brings newness, hope, and life. All things are beautiful and often rains a lot, it gets warmer, but the nights are cold, and light jackets are worn during this time. The snow begins to melt and chirping can be heard from birds returning from the south. The trees and flowers start to bloom; the air is fresh, but the pollen affects those with allergies, while some develop new allergies. More people are seen outside as it begins to get warm.

Like in any other country, summer can be very hot. Since Canadians often experience cold weather, many complain about the heat because it is not something they are accustomed to. People enjoy the outdoors during this time, hiking or picnics in the parks and by the lakes. There are a lot of trails and provincial parks, and usually, these places are bustling. Families enjoy picnics anywhere outside as I was surprised when I saw a family outside a fast-food restaurant enjoying their picnics. I admire how Canadians explore the outdoors during Summer, it is also a popular time for barbeques.

Other popular activities include families visiting their cottages and camping with trailers at designated campsites. Summer is from June to September and wished summer would last longer. The evenings can begin feeling chilly in late August. I will never forget our first summer; it remained warm until September.

As the months progress, it gets cooler and fall begins. This is an amazingly beautiful season when before the leaves fall from the trees onto the ground they change into beautiful colors like red, yellow and brown. The first snow can come in November, I experienced snow when we relocated to Alberta in October.

CHAPTER 9
WORK OPPORTUNITIES

Troy had to wait until I started school and got an admission letter before applying for his work permit. By then, he was out of vacation mode and ready to start his life in Canada. We started to apply for jobs while his permit was processed. His resume' was placed on a job site, and within a few days, a recruiter contacted him. He was invited to an interview and a tour of the company. The interview was successful. Troy was advised that he would not be able to receive any time off until the probation period was completed. He informed them that he was awaiting his permit and social security number, he was advised that he had to have those documents before being employed and the employer promised to hold the job until Troy received the documents.

In October 2018, Troy's mom, who had been ailing for some time, passed away as her condition worsened. Her passing was a very traumatic and challenging time for our family. We had just moved to Canada and hoped to connect and spend quality time with her since she lived here most of the time. We had not yet adjusted to our new surroundings but now had to deal with such a sorrowful situation and her funeral planning. I was surprised by how Troy handled his mother's passing. He was sorrowful but displayed strength for his siblings and our children. I had a close relationship with her but had to be strong for him, his siblings and our children.

When we told our children their grandma had passed, G as we affectionately call our daughter broke down in tears and ran to call my mom, who consoled her. Nathan asked, "Why are you all crying? Don't you know that Grandma has gone to Heaven?" "The innocence of children"

We received tremendous support from family, friends, and the church community. We laid our mom to rest and continued our lives where we had left off.

We thought God's timing was perfect when Troy's work permit was issued a month after his mother's passing. By now, it was almost the end of the year, so the employer who had offered him the job previously asked him to begin working in the new year.

He was excited to start his Canadian job, but after a month, he began complaining about back pains, as his body was not accustomed to this strenuous type of work. The job was in a metal plant where he had to stand for twelve hours a day lifting heavy metals. His work shifts were from 7am to 7 pm or 7 pm to 7 am daily, with three days off. He had thought that because he got the days off, it would be easier on his body, and was depressed whenever he had to return to work. I empathized with him, especially when he had to do those long night shifts. We decided to purchase a car when I completed school, since he worked in close proximity to home and could take the bus or Uber occasionally.

Budgeting and a positive cash flow were vital for us, since I attended school and lived on one income. We were happy Troy was paid way above minimum wage so he could comfortably care for our family.

He was extremely stressed and was determined to quit his job. He cried sometimes when he had to go to work. His work environment was toxic; the "F-bomb" was used after every other word, and the older men were disrespectful to the younger men, even though they were not disrespectful toward him. Once an employee tried to disrespect him, Troy sternly looked at the man and said, "Is Jamaica me come from." From that time, no other employee tried to disrespect him. He complained that the workers often did not attend work regularly, which made his job harder because he had to do their jobs also. I knew he had a strong work ethic, but my admiration for him increased as he worked tirelessly for our family. Many times when he decided to quit his job, I encouraged him to persevere as he would soon get a better job.

My heart would pound very fast when he called me from work, as I was never sure if he was calling to say he had quit the job. This also became stressful for me since it affected him, but I had to keep my focus. There was no time for a pity party. We just had to cope until changes came.

Most manufacturing companies in Ontario are unionized, which means that they prioritize seniority when it comes to promotions, salary increases, and bonuses. A few days before Troy's first anniversary, the company gave a bonus but did not include him because his timing was short a few days for the period. HR and his manager wanted to give it to him because of his hard work, dedication, and commitment, but the union would not approve it. He was most upset because he wanted to use the funds towards my last term's semester fee.

I called my confidant Alecia and asked her to agree in prayer with me about the situation. We prayed and asked the Lord to give him favour with the union to get the increase and bonus. I didn't tell him we prayed and two weeks later, he told me a notice was displayed to override the previous information. He received his bonus and remained at that job for three years.

International students were allowed to work full-time during semester breaks. My school friend Suzette accompanied me to an agency to sign up for a job. The only available work was at a factory; when I told Troy and my mom that I accepted the job, they laughed at me. They said they could not imagine me in that environment. Troy told me he would be surprised if I lasted the day on the job. Before we had left Jamaica, I told the Lord I would do any job; just don't give me a position where I have to clean toilets.

I was very excited to start the job because I had never done this type of work before although, I was paid minimum wage. It was only thirty minutes away from home by car, but it was one hour by bus. I had to take two buses or one bus and an Uber or one bus and walk for twenty minutes. After a while, commuting became more accessible, as my co-workers would offer me a ride.

The first assignment on the job was to place labels on the center of lotion bottles. There was a technique to do this. I was expected to master the task by midday, which I did not. I just could not get it! The supervisor picked on me and asked where was I from, when I told her Jamaica, she asked, "So why has everyone else mastered the task, but you can't get it?"

I told her it was my first time doing this type of job and I was trying my best. She didn't care; she just wanted me to do it right. The factory environment was no different from school; it was a mixture of nationalities. The supervisor and another senior woman were Jamaicans. The senior woman Claire, guided me and told me the do's and don'ts of the environment. The main thing she told me was to do my work and do not talk with anyone. She didn't have to advise me about that because I could not master the task much more to be talking to others to draw attention to myself.

The supervisor watched me keenly while I worked. I had to work quickly and complete the task accurately. I would get some of the labels right and She would call me out when I got them wrong. My new norm was to pray under my breath while I worked as I wanted to keep the job to make up my school fee for the last semester.

When we moved to the next task of making boxes, the older Jamaican woman Claire would help me in the supervisor's absence; she would start the boxes for me then I would finish them. She was experienced as she had worked at the factory on several occasions. As soon as the supervisor approached Claire would quickly run back to her station. The tasks changed throughout my three months there. I wasn't perfect at any task, but I remained there until my time expired. I was grateful for the opportunity and experience. I now have a greater respect for factory workers. It wasn't easy standing for eight hours.. It was amusing how the workers stopped their tasks and rang to lunch or at break time and at the end of the work day. I thought I could never survive this job as a permanent worker. Some of the workers were accustomed to this environment, whilst others like myself, were not. It was mostly immigrants such as nurses, engineers, accountants, chemists, and students waiting to do their master's programs worked at the factory.

A job is just a job in Canada; it does not define who you are. People seldomly ask what type of work you do when you meet them.

Students had the opportunity of delivering newspapers in the neighbourhood. G and several of her friends did that some days after school. It included putting the papers together and delivered them to houses in the area. The residents paid them for this service. She was happy to make her own money, and I liked her sense of responsibility.

CHAPTER 10
THE INTERVIEWS

I did not have all the funds for my last semester. At the end of the term, I visited the accounts office to inquire if I could pay a portion now and the balance later. This was not a popular option because students were expected to have their entire school fee when they entered the program. When the bursar asked when I would pay the balance, I boldly told him by the end of January. I had yet to determine where the balance would come from at that time, but I believed something would work out.

Around mid-January, I received an email from Canada Revenue Agency saying that they had miscalculated my taxes and owed me money. They sent the breakdown of the amount and when I would receive it. The amount owed to me was around three hundred dollars, just short of what I owed on my school fee. I was in awe! I left school having paid off all my school fees!

Many international students believe they should file their taxes until they start working in the country. This is not so; taxes should be filed as soon as you come into the country and they are due. There are a lot of benefits derived from filing your taxes, especially if you have children. Students are usually low on the income scale and will usually qualify for child tax benefits, which can become a source of income.

The unexpected happened in March, only one month before I completed my studies. The pandemic! We finished our classes online, including exams. This was a relatively easy transition because we were familiar with doing our exams online in the classroom.

We didn't get an in-person graduation; they just did a recording with the names of the graduates and the programs they did.

School ended, and it was time to secure a job. My thoughts were, how will I secure a job in a pandemic? How is this going to work out? People are losing jobs. Who was going to hire me? I needed clarification about which field I would search for, since my work experience differed from myqualifications. How was I going to make this transition? I thought.

My professors guided me on how to transition, but I was still trying to decide which career field I would search for. A college friend, who did the same programs, advised me on possible areas to explore. That gave me a push start and then I focused only on that field.

For an international student, Immigration Canada has specific requirements about the job category you can work in to renew your spouse's work permit.

The first job I applied for, I got an interview. They did the initial and second interviews on the same day, hours apart. I chose that option. The recruiter advised me if I passed the interview, she would contact me the following morning. A day passed, and I heard nothing from them. I woke up the next morning crying. I was crying because I felt like I had failed my family. My husband was relying on me to get this job so his permit could be extended. I fell into depression immediately. My husband was surprised to see me crying.

He asked what was wrong. I told him I failed; I did not get the job. He said that was okay. I was inconsolable. I cried out to the Lord! "Lord, I need a word from you!" As I took up the Bible, it opened to Isaiah 43. My attention was immediately drawn to verses 19-20: I will make a pathway through the wilderness. I will create rivers in the dry wasteland. The wild animals in the fields will thank me, the jackals and owls, too, for giving them water in the desert. Yes, I will make rivers in the dry wasteland so my chosen people can be refreshed. My tears dried up instantly; my Lord had spoken. I only needed to trust him.

During my job search a few days later, the same company kept popping up in my feed. I said, I am not sure why this keeps appearing, but I am going to apply. A few days later, I was out with my brother's wife when I saw an email come in from the company. They wanted to interview me. I was surprised! I answered and agreed to the time they suggested.

The phone interview went great! The Human Resources manager interviewed me. After the interview, I sent her a thank you email. She responded and informed me that I was selected for another interview with her and the unit manager.

During that time, I received invitations for interviews from two other companies. I got accepted for one of the jobs, but I declined the offer because it did not suit the immigration requirement.

A few days later, I did a Zoom interview with the company. It went very well. Troy was home and heard me do the interview. When I finished, he said, "Baby, that job is yours."

I sent a thank you email to the HR manager within minutes, and she responded with a job offer! Wow, the same job I had been rejected for before. The start date was on my birthday. I could not contain myself! What a birthday gift! I was even more excited because this company is one of the largest companies in its category in North America and was awarded for eight consecutive years as the best employer in Canada! This company met ninety-nine percent of the criteria I was looking for. I was in good hands!

On the same day, I was invited to interview with another top company, which I declined.

I was in awe! Look what the Lord had done! In the middle of the pandemic, he made a way for me! He blessed me with a job where I did not have to clean toilets! According to what I asked him.

I took up my Bible to read Isaiah 43:19-20 and to praise God, but instead, without realizing it, I turned to Isaiah 41: 17-20:

When the poor and needy search for water and there is none,
   and their tongues are parched from thirst,
then I, the LORD, will answer them.
   I, the God of Israel, will never abandon them.
I will open up rivers for them on the high plateaus.
   I will give them fountains of water in the valleys.
I will fill the desert with pools of water.
   Rivers fed by springs will flow across the parched ground.
I will plant trees in the barren desert—

cedar, acacia, myrtle, olive, cypress, fir, and pine.
I am doing this so all who see this miracle
  will understand what it means—
that it is the LORD who has done this,
  the Holy One of Israel who created it.

Whilst reading this passage, I recognized that it was a different passage! I realized that it connected with the first scripture I had read.

I brought it to my husband's attention, and he agreed! We were amazed!

I told one of my college colleagues, who wanted a job in the special category. Like myself, she applied and got through. She was scheduled to begin a month later.

I went into the office on the first day to meet my manager and collect my laptop and other resources. A license was required for the position, and I had to sit the exam in two and a half weeks.

I was required to read two and a half books with over two hundred pages each, except for one, which was half the size of one. How could I do this? It was not possible! Throughout my college and university life, I had never completed reading a textbook. And now I had to complete this in two weeks.

I celebrated my birthday. Then, I began reading the day after.

I was required to do self-learning. In the mornings, a general training session was held online. This required disciple, sacrifice, and commitment. I felt like I was back in school again, glued down to the computer and these books. I never complained because passing this exam was essential to keeping the job.

One thing was clear: even when we pray, and God answers our prayers, we have to play our part. We do the natural, and he will do the supernatural to make things work for us.

Whilst in training one morning, I asked a question, and a Jamaican by the name of Nicole, recognized the Jamaican accent. She messaged me privately, and we decided to study together.

During my time of studies, my family went on trips and did a lot of fun activities. They begged me to come with them sometimes, but I told them this was temporary, only two weeks; then, I would be free to live my life again.

The exam day came, and I was very nervous but believed I would be successful. I prayed, "Lord, please write this exam for me because that's the only way I will pass." When I started the exam, I smiled to myself. I was familiar with a lot of the questions from studying. As I progressed, the questions became harder. I finally completed the two-hour exam. The score could be accessed immediately. I was scared to open it. Donna called me to find out how it went. I told her I was nervous to look at my score. She stayed on the phone with me while I accessed the score. I was successful! I got two marks over the pass mark! Praise God! Another hurdle won!

The training lasted for six weeks. I learned a lot but was concerned about how to succeed at this job because it was so much information.

This was an amazing company, and I enjoyed my job! Management, my team, and the benefits were great. I was happy at my new job; it was perfect for me.

My first evaluation was good! My manager was impressed and told me if I continued the good work, then I would be an outstanding employee. Needless to say, I continued in the same manner and was rewarded accordingly.

My college friend, who guided me into that career path, expressed that her job was getting harder, and she was annoyed. I said, "Girl, why should you be stressing out yourself? Don't you know I can help you!" I recommended her for a position at my work, and she was successful. Another family friend, who had not worked for over fifteen years, was also recommended for the job and was successful. Another friend of mine, doing a career change recommended her, and she was also successful. I thought it seemed like the Lord had positioned me at this company to help all these people. Today, they are all still working with the company.

CHAPTER 11
DID I MAKE THE RIGHT DECISION

During the pandemic, I had a few low moments. One was when I lost my beloved uncle. On the other hand, I was also tremendously blessed. I experienced many high moments. I graduated from university and college, I received my "dream job," and our daughter was valedictorian and received the Ontario Principal's Award, among other accomplishments.

Canada is the second-largest country in the world and is always welcoming immigrants. Whilst this is true, one has to be strategic to be successful. There are various ways to become a Permanent Resident. However, the responsibility is on individuals to prepare and to do proper research to be successful, especially if you decide to live in Ontario, which is the most popular and competitive province. Most people settle there because of their support system.

I knew it would take a miracle under normal circumstances outside of COVID-19 to live in Ontario and be successful with our Permanent Resident status, simply because once you are above a certain age, it becomes more competitive. Other credentials does not matter. Nevertheless, we had a plan B: to move to the Atlantic Province the following summer, where the immigration process was more favorable. Due to the program they have to live and work there for a year. This program catered to people up to age fifty five.

I met ten Christian ladies whilst in college. I believe we were all connected through divine intervention. We formed a group to encourage and intercede for each other in prayer. During the pandemic, since most of us completed school and were in quarantine, we decided to meet on Zoom to have morning prayers. One of the things we prayed about was that immigration legislation would change in our favor, so we could receive our Permanent Residence.

Less than a year after, Immigration Refugees and Citizenship Canada (IRCC) did a historic draw with a score of seventy-five points! They selected over twenty-three thousand candidates! Once you are in Canada and in the express entry pool, and once you have Canadian work experience, you are selected. This was a day of Jubilee! One person in our intercessory group met the criteria and was selected! We were elated for her.

Two months later, Immigration, Refugees and Citizenship Canada (IRCC) announced the Temporary Resident to Permanent Resident pathway (TR to PR pathway). This was a new pathway to Permanent Residency for over 90,000 essential workers and international graduates already in Canada. Mighty God! It was happening! The Lord was answering our prayers!

A number of us from our group successfully applied. Two months after we were offered PR again through the express entry program! We now had options. I declined the letter because the first program required less documentation, and it was already being processed. I just had to wait on the approval. We waited in contentment.

As I saw things come together, I recalled, six months after we had arrived in Canada, when my mind had been attacked by the thought, what have you done, to move with your family here without being certain if things will work out? My heart started to beat fast, and it felt so true and real. For around a week, I walked around in despair. Then one morning during my devotion, the Lord had me turn in the Bible to Galatians 3:1-5 (NIV).

You foolish Galatians! Who has bewitched you? Before your very eyes Jesus Christ was clearly portrayed as crucified. I would like to learn just one thing from you: Did you receive the Spirit by the works of the law, or by believing what you heard? Are you so foolish?

After beginning by means of the Spirit, are you now trying to finish by means of the flesh? Have you experienced so much in vain—if it really was in vain? So again I ask, does God give you his Spirit and work miracles among you by the works of the law, or by your believing what you heard? So also Abraham "believed God, and it was credited to him as righteousness."

Understand, then, that those who have faith are children of Abraham. Scripture foresaw that God would justify the Gentiles by faith, and announced the gospel in advance to Abraham: "All nations will be blessed through you." So those who rely on faith are blessed along with Abraham, the man of faith.

I was surprised by how precise this passage of scripture was to the situation I was experiencing. I did not recall ever reading it before.

I laid on my belly and wept! I repented and asked the Lord for forgiveness.

"How could I be so stupid? Why did I allow Satan to attack my mind? You have been leading and directing me, and all things were working together. I started out in faith but was now depending on my efforts to complete the journey. I had experienced so much favor and goodness. No, Lord it was not in vain. You have been working by your spirit, and I thank you. I believe all that you told me. I will walk by faith, Lord. Sorry, I will not do it again." That was the first and last time I doubted and mistrusted the Lord about our journey.

One day, after the pandemic had started, I was surprised to receive a text from our landlord that something had come up and they needed the place. I was in shock! The thoughts of what, how can we move during this time. We are in quarantine! I believe there was honesty and transparency so why was not a question?

I was confused about how this was going to work. Troy and I had met with them and acknowledged the explanation but asked if grace could be extended to us.

At that point, I had just graduated and started job hunting. We were still on one income. That was enough trouble for us at that time. We could not possibly handle anything more. By now, we also needed our own vehicle to move around.

We explained our situation, and they obliged. We were grateful for the extension. We honestly could not give a definitive time when we could leave but kept updating them, as promised, as our situation changed.

Troy was still commuting on the bus during COVID when we decided it would be safer if he had his own vehicle. Also, since I would get a job soon, we could afford to purchase a vehicle.

During his search, he saw a vehicle that he thought would be a good fit for us. When he went to view the vehicle, the seller told him that she had already promised to sell it to a man who contacted her earlier in the day but that if he changed his mind, he would be considered. Later that day, she contacted him to let him know the vehicle was sold. Two weeks later, during his search, he came across a similar vehicle. We decided to go view it. The owner said he had only had it for two weeks because he bought it for his granddaughter, but the insurance was too costly. We decided to take the vehicle. After we returned home, it occurred to my husband that it was the same vehicle he had viewed recently. He was convinced that it was the same one because he remembered a particular scratch he had seen on the first vehicle and there was the same scratch on this one.

When we returned to pick up the vehicle, it was the original vehicle that he had wanted to purchase. The registration was in the previous owner's name with the address he had visited prior. This marveled us.

This proved a popular saying in Jamaica to be true: "If it is yours, it cannot be not for you." It seemed as though we were destined to be the owners of that vehicle.

We began the search for a new home when we were financially capable and the quarantine had lifted. The rental prices were ridiculously high. We preferred to rent somewhere where we did not have to share any amenities, nor did we want to move our children from their school. However, we did not limit our search. We found nothing convenient for us. By this time, we had asked that our time be extended until the end of the school term.

We got professional help, help from family and friends, but we could not find a suitable place, except one, which we were going to put an offer on, but it was too expensive. The day after, we crunched the figures again. We decided to withdraw the offer because it would be too strenuous to afford that rent. We prayed, but no doors were opening for us to find a new home in Ontario.

CHAPTER 12
DESTINY & TIME MET

It was now almost the end of the children's school term. I overheard Troy and Judy speaking on the phone, saying it might be better if we moved out to Alberta. I laughed to myself and thought, no way am I moving there.

He came and asked, how did I feel about moving to Alberta? I told him no. It wasn't a good idea because the children were settled in Ontario they had developed close relationships with our families and their friends, and I felt the same way.

I did not want to leave because I was comfortable and at peace with my surroundings. I developed a fantastic relationship with Dave and Donna and my niece Tianna. Although I had other families in Ontario, I was not close to them. Dave and his family were my only close family in Canada. We prayed and asked the Lord if this is a move we should make. We sought counsel, and the answer was a resounding, yes, go.

I still did not want to leave Ontario. I felt a release to go to Alberta after I spoke with Dave he told me, "Sis, do what is best for you and your family. You came here with a goal. You did not come to Canada to be working until retirement age in this cold." **He said this because housing and living expenses are more affordable in Alberta. The tax on goods and services is less than in Ontario. Toronto and British Colombia are two of Canada's most expensive cities, and families often move to other Provinces.**

My employer, at the time, operated in four provinces. When I inquired if there was any availability for a transfer to Alberta, I was told one spot was available. It seemed that one space was reserved for me by the Lord. I spoke to the manager in Alberta. She was excited to have me on her team; the rest was history.

I told Troy, let's go! My heart was sad to leave; it was not my desire to go, but we had to. We could not find a suitable home in Ontario. Our children did not take the news of us relocating well. They came up with several reasons why we should not leave, including that they had developed friendships, they would miss their Uncle Dave, Auntie Donna and their cousin Tianna, and would not see Bryanna (Dave's and Donna's daughter, who lives in the

United States) when she visited and Jayden (Donna's nephew), Uncle Leon and Auntie Vennessa, Dominique and Shawntee, were the main reasons they stated. Nathan, who was seven years old then, said if we were not moving into our own home, we should not go; he said it did not make sense to relocate and live in a rented house. He gave in after a while without any fuss when Troy and I comforted him by telling him that we would buy him a basketball hoop outside our house when we moved to Alberta. (he loves basketball and always wanted a hoop.) We would also have preferred moving into our home, but it was not time.

Gihannah cried inconsolably the night before we left Ontario. Her friends were in disbelief that she was leaving Ontario, and about four of her friends gathered outside the townhouse and wept. My heart was broken for them, but we had no choice but to leave.

Troy told Judy to start looking for housing for us. She found a townhouse for us around the third place that she viewed. It was perfect! The location and amenities were all within walking distance. I believe the Lord always knows how to put a smile on his children's faces. One of their favourite fast-food places was a three-minute walk from our townhouse. We had more than enough space at this house and would pay half of the amount of money we paid for rent in Ontario..

When we decided to relocate, Troy was relieved because he was leaving his strenuous job, he proceeded to Alberta two weeks before us. I hadn't seen my husband this happy since we moved to Canada. He headed this transition; I was just following his lead.

As I was on the plane to Alberta, I tried to hold back the tears, but I felt them rolling down my cheeks. I was happy G and Nate was sleeping because I was not in the frame of mind to explain why I was crying. I did not know how to express my emotions verbally. Although I was at peace relocating, I thought this was not my plan. I did not know if I was supposed to be happy, but I was unafraid. I wanted to live in this moment privately to reflect. I was now on a new journey to complete the journey which started seven years before. I was confident this time would be different and our journey of making Canada our permanent home would be complete. The Lord was finishing what He had started. I was overwhelmed by my emotions.

Troy and Judy picked us up from the airport. He looked happy and comfortable at home. As we drove home, I sat quietly in the back of the vehicle with our children. I was still in a reflective mood. I was once more captivated by the beauty of Alberta, the fresh air, expansive land space, and lush greenery. It was peaceful, and it was nothing like city life in Ontario.

When we arrived at Judy's house, the children were surprised by their Uncle Leon and Aunty Vennessa, who had flown in from Toronto a few days before we arrived. Their presence brought happiness for G and Nate, and they were excited that their aunt and uncle had come to support us.

We settled into our new home without any eventualities. The children were excited about our new home. They loved that they had a lot more space and would live close to their aunt. I remained in a reflective mood for some time. We enjoyed the rest of the summer doing fun activities as a family, exploring the city, and visiting new home developments.

My daughter was apprehensive about the new school year because she thought most of the students would already know each other, and it would be hard to meet new friends. My son, on the other hand, was excited to go to his new school. They adjusted well and made new friends.

We were excited about our first Thanksgiving because some friends from Ontario joined us. Melissa, whom I met at Centennial College & her husband decided to move to Alberta after I sent videos of the new home developments and the beautiful landscape. My friend, Nicole, from work, relocated a month after I moved. I was elated to have them because I thought it was important to have friends close to me...

Time passed, and we received no information from Immigration Canada about our applications. We continued to pray that it would be process quickly, Not that there were any threats of not getting it soon, but we thought it was time for us to receive our Permanent Residence..

I decided to visit some of the places where I made declarations years ago while in Alberta and ask the Lord to release our Permanent Resident documents. I kept doing this until four months later, when we received an email that our applications were being processed, and they needed additional documentation. We were elated to hear from them and sent the document within the required time.

Finally, in the third month of the eighth year of our journey in pursuit to live in Canada, we received our approval for Permanent Resident! In the Bible, the number three means divine perfection, and eight means prosperity & new beginnings. This was Jubilation! The word of the Lord had come to pass! Mark 11:22-23, Psalm 16:6, Isaiah 43:19-20 and so many other scriptures through which he had spoken to me.

This may not be a big deal for someone who has never wanted to live outside of their country of birth or anyone who has never decided to pursue a dream and it come through.

Our journey has proven that if anyone has a desire, commit it to the Lord and seeks His direction. He will give them the desires of their heart according to His will.

Nekeisha, one of my friends whom I had met at Orientation my first day at Centennial College, also moved with her family and her nephew Akeem followed her within a year of us moving to Alberta. They came to survey the area six months after I moved to Alberta and sent them video of new development. They went back to Ontario and began planning their move. The rest was history. Nekeisha has become one of my inner circle friend and business associates.

Another friend Nastacia that I met at Orientation also moved with her family two years after I moved. When I told her I was relocating she said "that's a big move" because Alberta is said to be colder than Ontario because of the mountains and its four hours plane ride from Ontario. "I said girl the big move was when we moved from Jamaica to Canada, we can now occupy any part of the land in Canada." She is also one of my business associates.

Another friend Denise I met at school who was part of our intercessory prayer group and got the job at the same company I worked, relocated a few weeks ago with her family. I know many more will continue to relocate to Alberta.

My friend Shara, I took under my wings as my little sister lives in another major city three hours away. She moved to Alberta as soon as she left school and was excited when I moved here. My family are excited when we go to that city because we get to see her.

I have met some amazing families while in Alberta that have become family mainly Collia nad Suzette. Our multi-nationed church family is fantastic. From the first day we visited, our pastor's son Theo and Nathan started a friendship which has grown.

Our church home and the organizations that I sought for a job on my first attempt to migrate to Canada is located along the same street.

It is the same street the employer said "sorry ma'am you will need a special permit."

It is the same street when I called Troy to say its not going to work for me to remain in Canada and he told me about the song "if it did not work the first time will you still try again? Will you still trust the Lord?"

It is amazing how the power of Lord Jesus Christ works.

Each time I go to church and pass the same company. I am reminded of my journey, and smiles. I tell my family don't get tired of hearing me say thank you Jesus! don't be ashame when I worship publicly. I am grateful for what the Lord has done for our family!

One of my dear friend Donna, from school connected me to Komal and Aman my business mentors. We are from two different cultures but we are family. Whenever I go to Ontario and we all go out together people are usually confused when Aman tell people we are family. We maybe of different cultures but respect each other's culture and share the love of curry and spice. God is love and living into a multi-cultured country has taught me to appreciate and embrace people of different cultures.

I am just amazed of God's faithful and awesomeness! Of how He carefully connects us with whomever he wants. There is always a purpose. He decides where we will live and the people we should be connected to. Some will be temporary relations whilst some are permanent. However, there is always a purpose. I am humbled.

I have seen what happens when I live my life in Christ Jesus. Whatever I have to offer the world through my gifts, talents, and business acumen, this book, if Jesus is not in it, is nothing.

Only when I allow Him to work through me for His glory does it count.

Galatians 2:20

> I have been crucified with Christ and I no longer live, but Christ lives in me. The life I now live in the body, I live by faith in the Son of God, who loved me and gave himself for me.

All honor, glory, and power belong to you, Christ Jesus.

JOURNAL YOU!

I am dedicating these next 3 pages to you. Now that you have read my story, this is your safe space to share your own thoughts about your plans to migrate. For those who have already migrated and still figuring out settling, it is good to take some time write your vision and make it plain.

_____

_____

_____

_____

_____

_____

_____

_____

Manufactured by Amazon.ca
Acheson, AB

15644152R00055